Musical MOVIE POSTERS

volume nine of
the illustrated history of movies through posters

Images from the Hershenson-Allen Archive

Previous Volumes:
Volume One: Cartoon Movie Posters
Volume Two: Cowboy Movie Posters
Volume Three: Academy Award Winners' Movie Posters
Volume Four: Sports Movie Posters
Volume Five: Crime Movie Posters
Volume Six: More Cowboy Movie Posters
Volume Seven: Horror Movie Posters
Volume Eight: Best Pictures' Movie Posters

Edited by Richard Allen and Bruce Hershenson
Published by Bruce Hershenson
P.O. Box 874, West Plains, MO 65775
Phone: (417) 256-9616 Fax (417) 257-6948
e-mail: mail@brucehershenson.com
website: http://www.brucehershenson.com

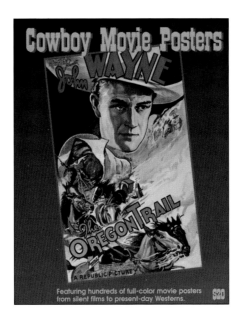

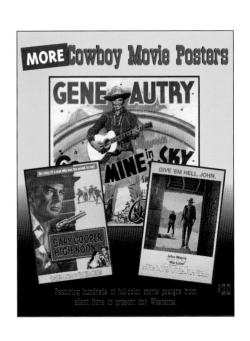

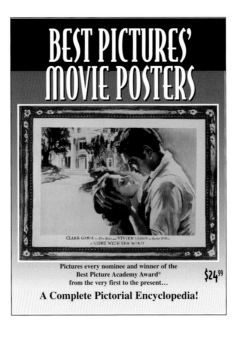

STILL AVAILABLE!

ORDER DIRECT

FROM THE PUBLISHER

OR CHECK YOUR

LOCAL BOOKSTORE. . .

IF THEY DON'T HAVE

THEM IN STOCK, THEY

CAN BE SPECIAL

ORDERED.

Introduction

Welcome to the ninth volume of The Illustrated History of Movies Through Posters. While the subject of this book, movie musicals, is one of the most popular genres of film, it is difficult to describe exactly what constitutes a musical. Most films have soundtracks, and many include a few musical numbers, but how much musical content does a film need before it is officially a musical? Since there are no clear-cut rules, I based this book on a few simple guidelines. First, I excluded all silent films, for obvious reasons. Second, I excluded movies where the musical numbers were not performed by the stars of the film, or movies that are basically comedies or dramas, but include a little music. Third, I excluded concert films or any films that did not have a plot. Finally, since this is a book of images, I tried to always give preference to posters that depict people singing or dancing.

However, on occasion I broke my own rules. In this series, I try to present a balance of films from all the years covered, so in years that were weak for musicals, I sometimes had to include lesser choices, and in other years that were strong for musicals I had to exclude many worthwhile posters. The period from 1933 to 1943 was so filled with musicals that I could easily devote a second volume entirely to images from those ten years alone!

Examining this book, it is clear that early movie musicals were dominated by a relatively small group of wonderful performers such as Alice Faye, Betty Grable, and, of course, Fred Astaire and Ginger Rogers. These stars worked primarily for 20th Century Fox and RKO, which often produced posters of remarkable beauty.

You will note that not all of the posters in this volume are of the original United States movie poster, called a one-sheet. I used other size posters either because I could not obtain the one-sheet image, or because I had already used it in another one of my volumes, or because I felt the image I used has superior graphics to the one-sheet image, or better conveys the idea of the film.

Unless otherwise noted, the image is of the original U.S. one-sheet poster, and measures 27" x 41". Other sizes included are lobby cards (11" x 14"), window cards (14" x 22"), inserts (14" x 36"), half-sheets (22" x 28"), three-sheets (41" x 81"), six-sheets (81" x 81"), twenty-four-sheets (9 ft x 20 ft), and foreign posters (varying sizes).

All the images in this book come from the Hershenson-Allen Archive. The archive consists of over 25,000 different movie poster images, all photographed directly from the original posters onto high quality 4" x 5" color transparencies. There is not another resource like it anywhere, and it is the world's foremost source of movie poster images. The Archive has provided images for books, videos, magazines, and newspapers.

This is not a catalog of posters for sale, nor do I sell any sort of movie poster reproductions! However, I do sell original movie posters of all sorts through public auctions and mail-order sales catalogs. If you are interested in acquiring original vintage movie posters (or any of the other books I have published) visit my website at http://www.bruce-hershenson.com (the most visited vintage movie poster site on the Internet, with hundreds of free images) and send me a self-addressed stamped envelope for free brochures.

I need to thank Amy Regez of Sullivan Santamaria Design who did the layouts and designed the covers for this book, and Sylvia Hershenson, who assisted in its preparation and did the proofreading. Most of all, I need to thank my partner, Richard Allen. He has always loved posters with beautiful graphics, and he contributed the lion's share of the images in this book. We share a common vision, and we hope to keep publishing these volumes until we have covered every possible genre of film.

I dedicate this book to my sons, Holden and Luke. In a few short years, they have added immeasurably to my life, and I believe the best is yet to be. Thanks, guys!

Bruce Hershenson
June 1999

1. THE JAZZ SINGER, 1927, twenty-four-sheet

2. THE SINGING FOOL, 1928, lobby card

3. THE BROADWAY MELODY, 1929, lobby card

4. BROADWAY BABIES, 1929, lobby card

5. HALLELUJAH, 1929, campaign book ad

6. GOLD DIGGERS OF BROADWAY, 1929,
window card

7. ON WITH THE SHOW, 1929, window card

8. FOX MOVIETONE FOLLIES, 1929, window card

9. TANNED LEGS, 1929

10. INNOCENTS OF PARIS, 1929, window card

11. THE DANCE OF LIFE, 1929

12. RIO RITA, 1929

13. SHOW BOAT, 1929

14. NO, NO, NANETTE, 1930

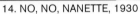

15. KING OF JAZZ, 1930, German poster

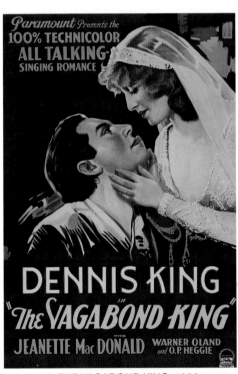

16. THE VAGABOND KING, 1930

17. WHOOPEE, 1930

18. ONE HOUR WITH YOU, 1932

19. FOOTLIGHT PARADE, 1933, window card

20. FLYING DOWN TO RIO, 1933

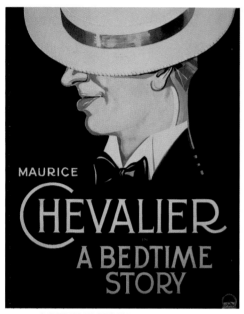

21. A BEDTIME STORY, 1933, window card

22. THE GOOD COMPANIONS, 1933

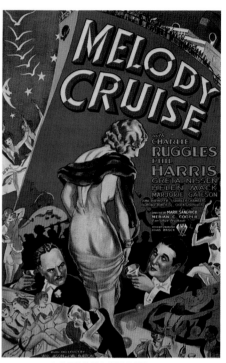

23. MELODY CRUISE, 1933

24. GOLD DIGGERS OF 1933, 1933, Title card

25. FOOTLIGHT PARADE, 1933, Title card

26. FLYING DOWN TO RIO, 1933, lobby card

27. FOOTLIGHT PARADE, 1933, lobby card

28. GOING HOLLYWOOD, 1933

29. 42ND STREET, 1933, Title card

30. 42ND STREET, 1933, lobby card

31. ROMAN SCANDALS, 1933

32. THE WAY TO LOVE, 1933

33. DANCING LADY, 1933, window card

34. KID MILLIONS, 1934, window card

35. SHE LOVES ME NOT, 1934

36. DOWN TO THEIR LAST YACHT, 1934, window card

37. BOLERO, 1934, lobby card

38. BABY, TAKE A BOW, 1934, Title card

39. GEORGE WHITE'S SCANDALS, 1934

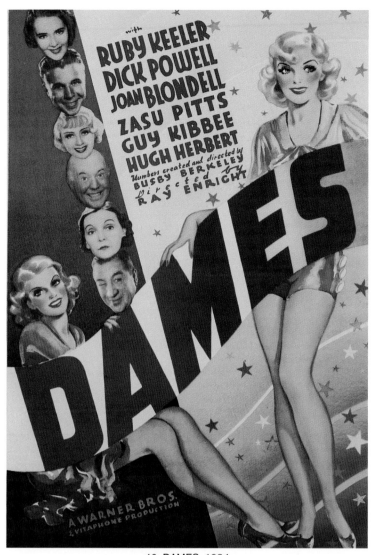

40. DAMES, 1934

41. THE GAY DIVORCEE, 1934

42. WAKE UP AND DREAM, 1934,
three-sheet

43. STAND UP AND CHEER, 1934

44. 20 MILLION SWEETHEARTS, 1934

45. KING OF BURLESQUE, 1935

46. GO INTO YOUR DANCE, 1935

47. NAUGHTY MARIETTA, 1935

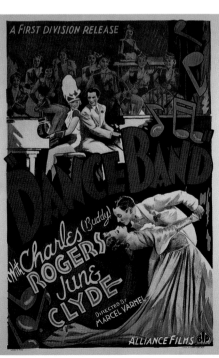

48. DANCE BAND, 1935

49. HOORAY FOR LOVE, 1935

50. ROBERTA, 1935

51. TOP HAT, 1935

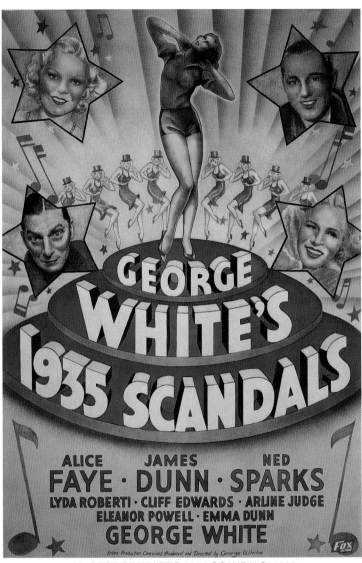

52. GEORGE WHITE'S 1935 SCANDALS, 1935

53. PARIS IN SPRING, 1935

54. THANKS A MILLION, 1935

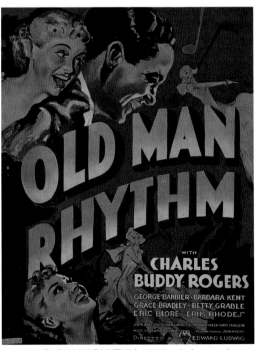

55. OLD MAN RHYTHM, 1935, window card

56. DANCING PIRATE, 1936

57. BORN TO DANCE, 1936, Leader Press

58. DIMPLES, 1936

59. ROSE MARIE, 1936, lobby card

60. SWING TIME, 1936, lobby card

61. FOLLOW THE FLEET, 1936

62. PENNIES FROM HEAVEN, 1936

63. SING BABY SING, 1936

64. THE SINGING KID, 1936

65. THE GREAT ZIEGFELD, 1936

66. SHOW BOAT, 1936

67. YOU'RE A SWEETHEART, 1937

68. SHALL WE DANCE, 1937

69. MOUNTAIN MUSIC, 1937

70. RHYTHM IN THE CLOUDS, 1937

71. YOU CAN'T HAVE EVERYTHING, 1937

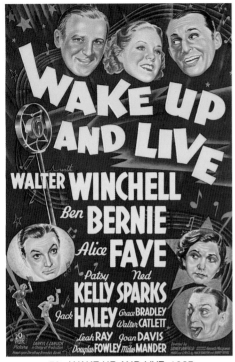

72 . WAKE UP AND LIVE, 1937

73. MAYTIME, 1937

74. SING AND BE HAPPY, 1937

75. ON THE AVENUE, 1937

76. TOP OF THE TOWN, 1937

77. ALEXANDER'S RAGTIME BAND, 1938

78. CAREFREE, 1938

79. COCOANUT GROVE, 1938

80. EVERYBODY SING, 1938

81. THE GREAT WALTZ, 1938

82. SALLY IRENE AND MARY, 1938

83. SING YOU SINNERS, 1938

84. LITTLE MISS BROADWAY, 1938

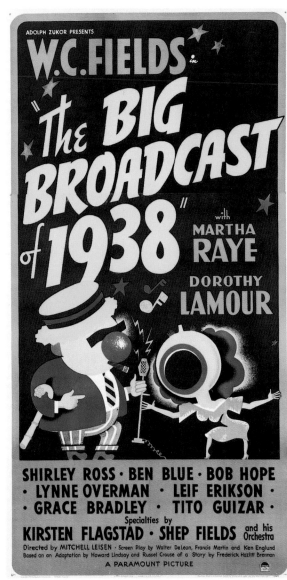

85. THE BIG BROADCAST OF 1938, 1938, three-sheet

86. MAD ABOUT MUSIC, 1938

87. THE STORY OF VERNON AND IRENE CASTLE, 1939

88. ST. LOUIS BLUES, 1939

89. SECOND FIDDLE, 1939

90. 3 SMART GIRLS GROW UP, 1939

91. THE THREE MUSKETEERS, 1939

92. THE GREAT VICTOR HERBERT, 1939

93. PARIS HONEYMOON, 1939

94. HONOLULU, 1939

95. ROSE OF WASHINGTON SQUARE, 1939

96. SWANEE RIVER, 1939, lobby card

97. BABES IN ARMS, 1939, lobby card

98. DOWN ARGENTINE WAY, 1940

99. TIN PAN ALLEY, 1940

100. STRIKE UP THE BAND, 1940

101. ROAD TO SINGAPORE, 1940

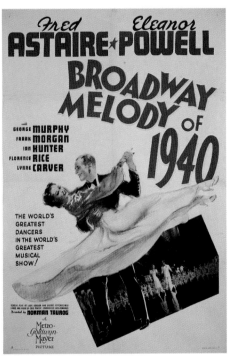

102. BROADWAY MELODY OF 1940, 1940

103. WEEK-END IN HAVANA, 1941

104. ZIEGFELD GIRL, 1941

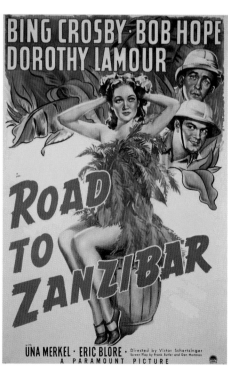

105. ROAD TO ZANZIBAR, 1941

106. RISE AND SHINE, 1941

107. LAS VEGAS NIGHTS, 1941

108. MOON OVER MIAMI, 1941

109. BABES ON BROADWAY, 1941

110. BIRTH OF THE BLUES, 1941

111. BLUES IN THE NIGHT, 1941

112. THAT NIGHT IN RIO, 1941

113. YOU'LL NEVER GET RICH, 1941

114. MY GAL SAL, 1942

115. SONG OF THE ISLANDS, 1942

116. HOLIDAY INN, 1942

117. FOOTLIGHT SERENADE, 1942

118. FOR ME AND MY GAL, 1942

119. ORCHESTRA WIVES, 1942

120. SING YOUR WORRIES AWAY, 1942

121. SYNCOPATION, 1942

122. YOU WERE NEVER LOVELIER, 1942

123. YANKEE DOODLE DANDY, 1942, Title card

124. YANKEE DOODLE DANDY, 1942, lobby card

125. SWEET ROSIE O'GRADY, 1943

126. CONEY ISLAND, 1943

127. THE GANG'S ALL HERE, 1943

128. PRESENTING LILY MARS, 1943

129. GIRL CRAZY, 1943

130. HAPPY GO LUCKY, 1943

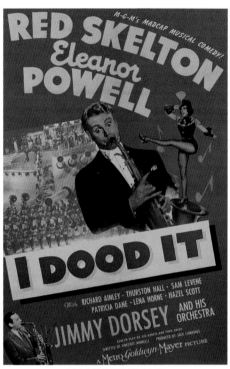

131. I DOOD IT, 1943

132. SALUTE FOR THREE, 1943

133. STORMY WEATHER, 1943

134. STORMY WEATHER, 1943, lobby card

135. CABIN IN THE SKY, 1943, lobby card

136. CABIN IN THE SKY, 1943

137. MEET ME IN ST. LOUIS, 1944

138. SWEET AND LOW-DOWN, 1944

139. MUSIC IN MANHATTAN, 1944

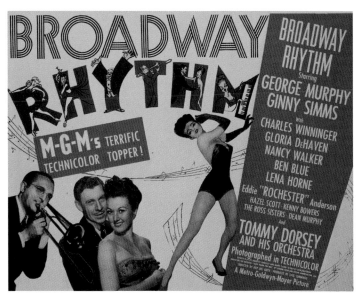

140. BROADWAY RHYTHM, 1944, Title card

141. SENSATIONS OF 1945, 1944, Title card

142. HIGHER AND HIGHER, 1944, Title card

143. STEP LIVELY, 1944, Title card

144. GREENWICH VILLAGE, 1944

145. COVER GIRL, 1944

146. SWING FEVER, 1944

147. SOMETHING FOR THE BOYS, 1944

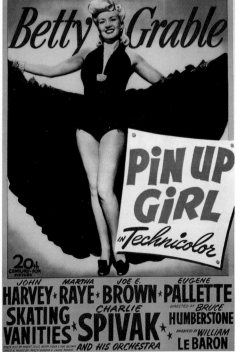

148. PIN UP GIRL, 1944

149. DIAMOND HORSESHOE, 1945

150. STATE FAIR, 1945

151. DOLL FACE, 1945

152. GEORGE WHITE'S SCANDALS, 1945

153. SING YOUR WAY HOME, 1945

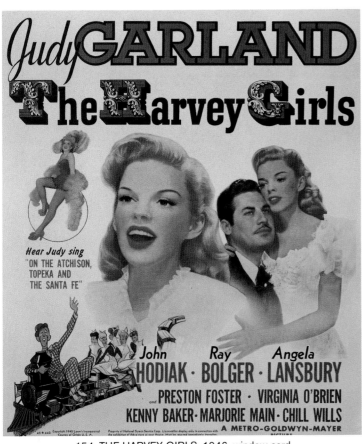

154. THE HARVEY GIRLS, 1946, window card

155. TILL THE CLOUDS ROLL BY, 1946

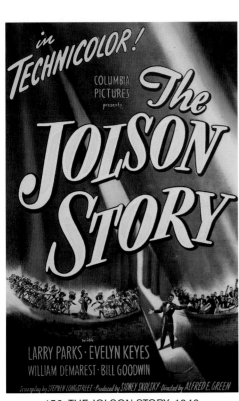

156. THE JOLSON STORY, 1946

157. ZIEGFELD FOLLIES, 1946, lobby card

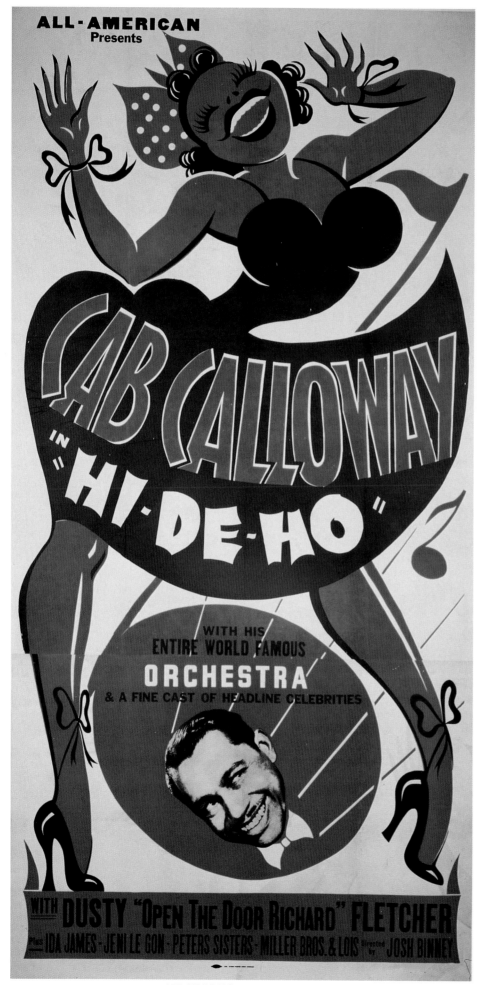

158. HI-DE-HO, 1947, three-sheet

159. BEAT THE BAND, 1947

160. IT HAPPENED IN BROOKLYN, 1947

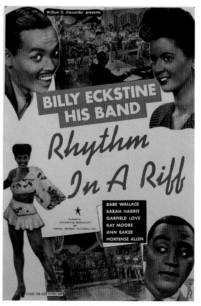

161. RHYTHM IN A RIFF, 1947

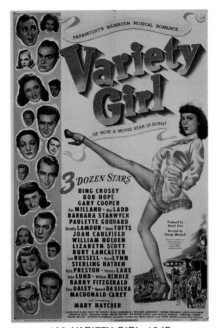

162. VARIETY GIRL, 1947

165. THE PIRATE, 1948, six-sheet

163. ON AN ISLAND WITH YOU, 1948

166. WORDS AND MUSIC, 1948, Title card

164. GIVE MY REGARDS TO BROADWAY,
1948

167. EASTER PARADE, 1948, Title card

168. THE EMPEROR WALTZ, 1948

169. WHEN MY BABY SMILES AT ME, 1948

170. HOLIDAY IN HAVANA, 1949

171. ON THE TOWN, 1949

172. YOU'RE MY EVERYTHING, 1949

173. WABASH AVENUE, 1950

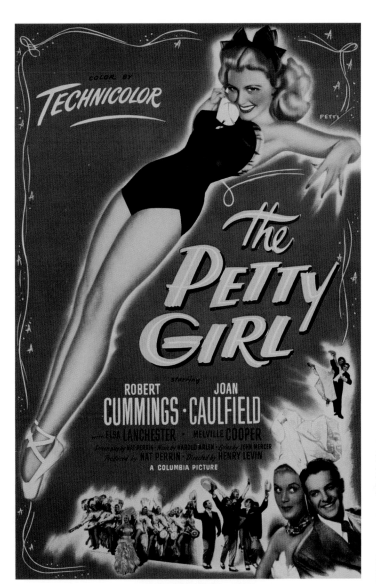

174. THE PETTY GIRL, 1950

175. MY BLUE HEAVEN, 1950

176. SUMMER STOCK, 1950

177. ANNIE GET YOUR GUN, 1950

178. AN AMERICAN IN PARIS, 1951, three-sheet

179. HAPPY GO LOVELY, 1951

180. ON MOONLIGHT BAY, 1951

181. ROYAL WEDDING, 1951

182. SINGIN' IN THE RAIN, 1952, lobby standee

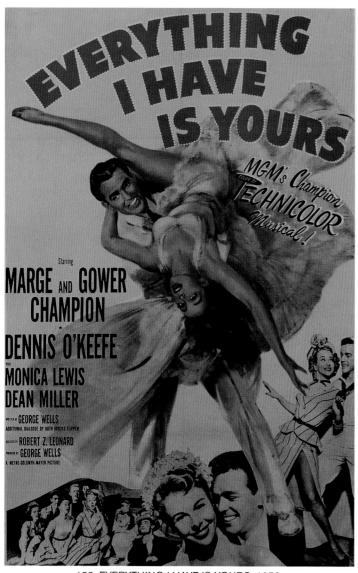

183. EVERYTHING I HAVE IS YOURS, 1952

184. WITH A SONG IN MY HEART, 1952, three-sheet

185. THE BELLE OF NEW YORK, 1952, Title card

186. STARS AND STRIPES FOREVER, 1952

187. GENTLEMEN PREFER BLONDES, 1953, Forty By Sixty

188. SO THIS IS LOVE, 1953

191. THE BAND WAGON, 1953, six-sheet

189. CALL ME MADAM, 1953

190. LATIN LOVERS, 1953

192. KISS ME KATE, 1953

193. BRIGADOON, 1954

194. THERE'S NO BUSINESS LIKE SHOW BUSINESS, 1954

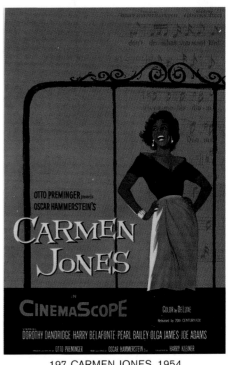

195. SEVEN BRIDES FOR SEVEN BROTHERS, 1954

196. A STAR IS BORN, 1954

197. CARMEN JONES, 1954

198. THE SEVEN LITTLE FOYS, 1955

199. OKLAHOMA, 1955

200. ROCK 'N' ROLL REVUE, 1955

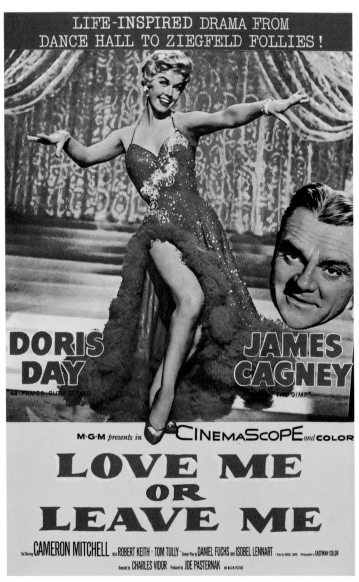

201. LOVE ME OR LEAVE ME, 1955

202. GUYS AND DOLLS, 1955

203. THE KING AND I, 1956, six-sheet

204. LOVE ME TENDER, 1956, three-sheet

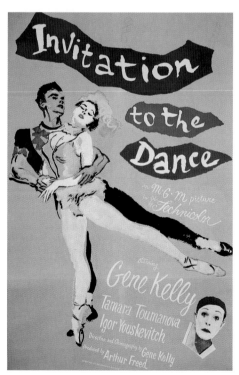

205. INVITATION TO THE DANCE, 1956

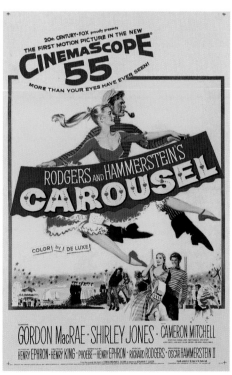

206. CAROUSEL, 1956

207. HIGH SOCIETY, 1956

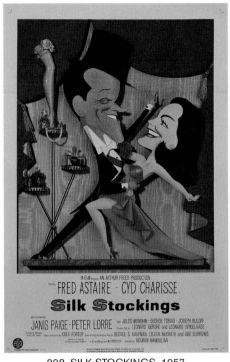

208. SILK STOCKINGS, 1957

209. APRIL LOVE, 1957

210. LES GIRLS, 1957

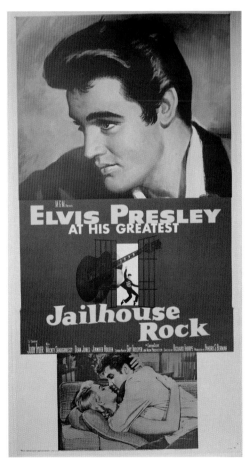

211. JAILHOUSE ROCK, 1957, three-sheet

212. FUNNY FACE, 1957, three-sheet

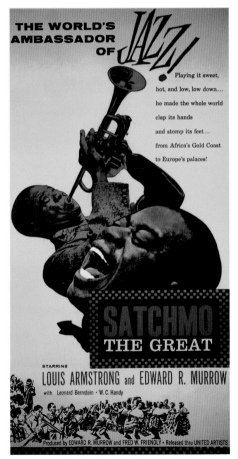

213. SATCHMO THE GREAT, 1957, three-sheet

214. GO, JOHNNY GO, 1958

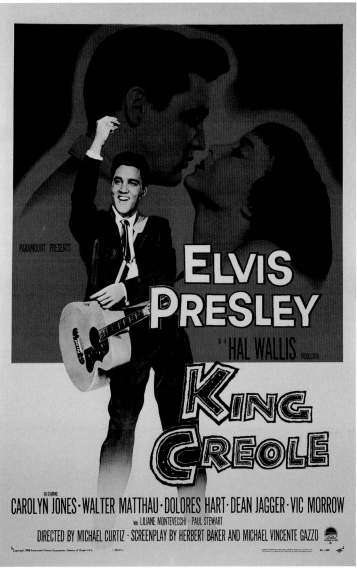

215. KING CREOLE, 1958

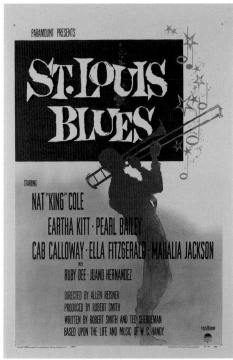

216. ST. LOUIS BLUES, 1958

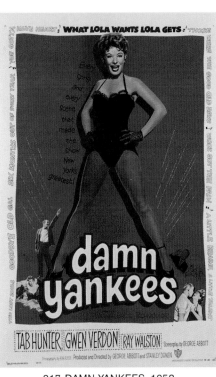

217. DAMN YANKEES, 1958

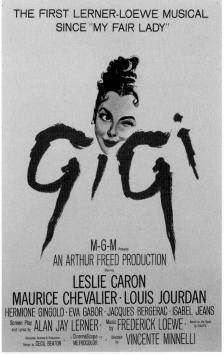

218. GIGI, 1958

219. PORGY AND BESS, 1959

220. THE FIVE PENNIES, 1959

221. G.I. BLUES, 1960, lobby card

222. CAN-CAN, 1960, Spanish poster

223. WEST SIDE STORY, 1961

224. THE MUSIC MAN, 1962, three-sheet

225. JUMBO, 1962

226. STATE FAIR, 1962

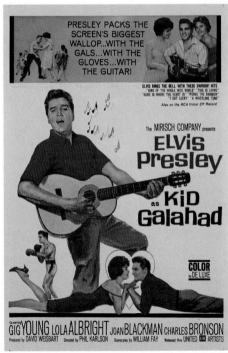

227. KID GALAHAD, 1962

228. BYE BYE BIRDIE, 1963

229. A HARD DAY'S NIGHT, 1964, lobby card

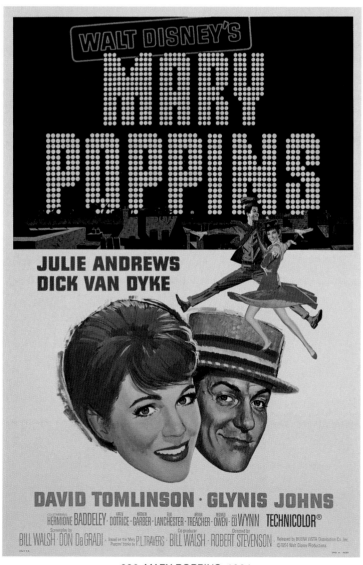

230. MARY POPPINS, 1964

231. MY FAIR LADY, 1964

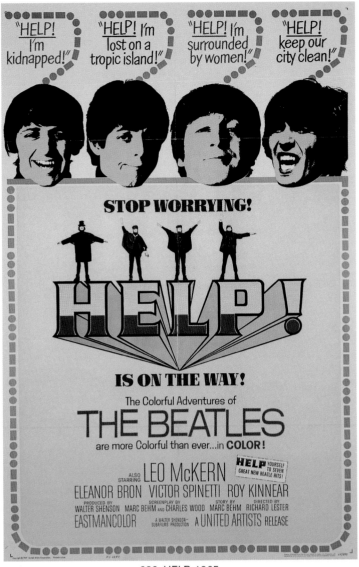

232. HELP!, 1965

233. HOLD ON, 1966

234. THE SOUND OF MUSIC, 1965, British Quad

235. THE SINGING NUN, 1966

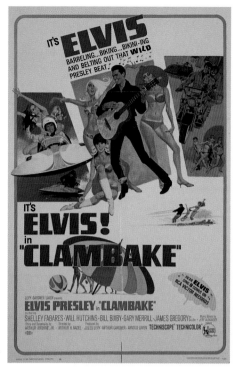

236. CLAMBAKE, 1967

237. GOOD TIMES, 1967

238. HALF A SIXPENCE, 1967

239. CAMELOT, 1967

240. THOROUGHLY MODERN MILLIE, 1967

241. HEAD, 1968

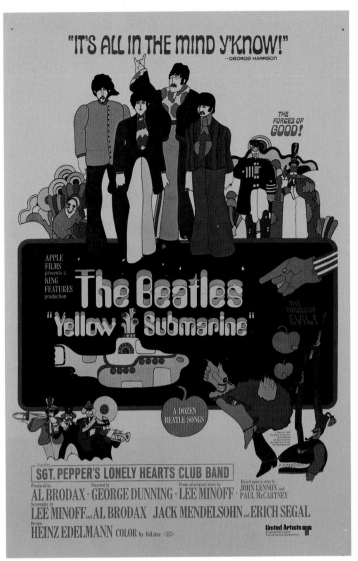

242. YELLOW SUBMARINE, 1968

243. OLIVER, 1968, half-sheet

244. FUNNY GIRL, 1968, three sheet

245. MRS. BROWN, YOU'VE GOT A LOVELY DAUGHTER, 1968

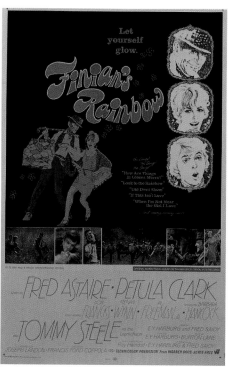

246. FINIAN'S RAINBOW, 1968

247. ALICE'S RESTAURANT, 1969

248. HELLO DOLLY, 1969

249. STAR, 1968

250. WOODSTOCK, 1970

251. ON A CLEAR DAY YOU CAN SEE FOREVER, 1970

252. THE BOY FRIEND, 1971

253. FIDDLER ON THE ROOF, 1971

254. WILLY WONKA AND THE CHOCOLATE FACTORY, 1971

255. LADY SINGS THE BLUES, 1972

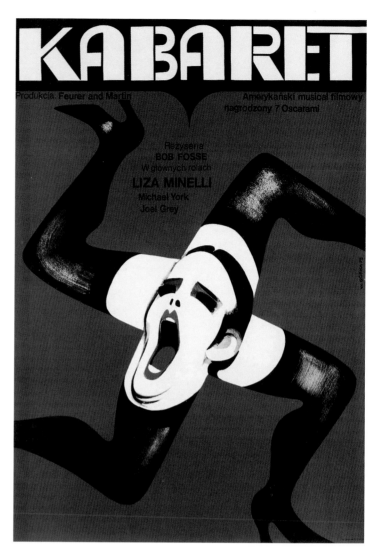

256. CABARET, 1972, Polish poster

257. MAN OF LA MANCHA, 1972

258. GODSPELL, 1973

259. LET THE GOOD TIMES ROLL, 1973

260. THAT'S ENTERTAINMENT, 1974

261. PHANTOM OF THE PARADISE, 1974

262. THE LITTLE PRINCE, 1974, insert

263. FUNNY LADY, 1975

264. NASHVILLE, 1975

265. AT LONG LAST LOVE, 1975

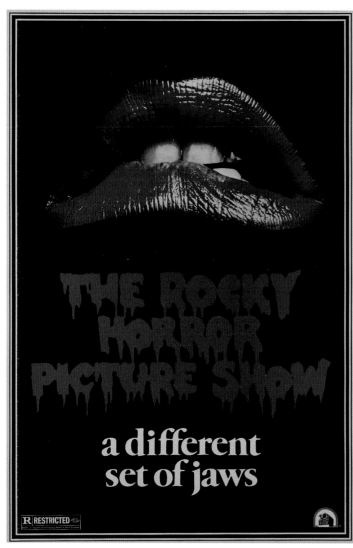

266. THE ROCKY HORROR PICTURE SHOW, 1975

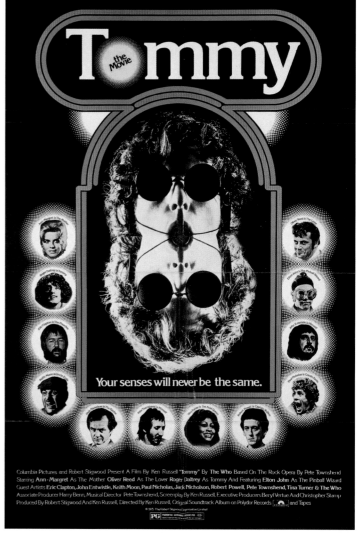

267. TOMMY, 1975

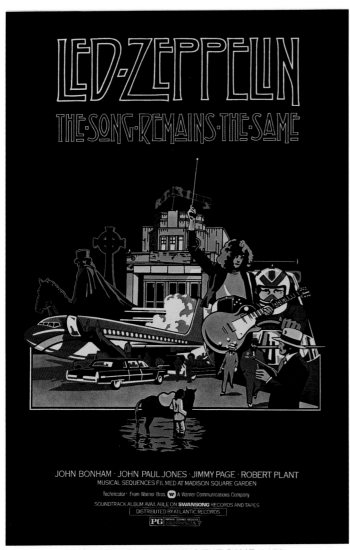

268. THE SONG REMAINS THE SAME, 1976

269. A STAR IS BORN, 1976

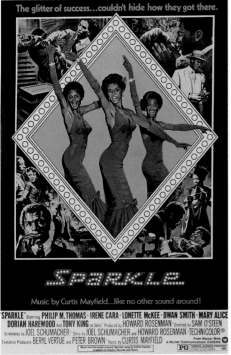

270. SPARKLE, 1976

271. BUGSY MALONE, 1976

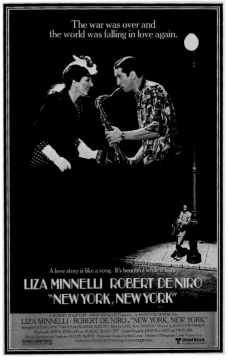

272. NEW YORK, NEW YORK, 1977

Catch it.

Opens December 16th at a theatre near you!

273. SATURDAY NIGHT FEVER, 1977

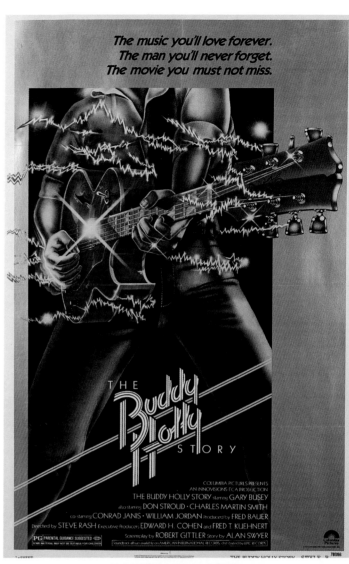

274. THANK GOD IT'S FRIDAY, 1978

275. THE BUDDY HOLLY STORY, 1978

276. DISCO FEVER, 1978

277. AMERICAN HOT WAX, 1978

278. THE WIZ, 1978

John Travolta   Olivia Newton-John

GREASE is the word

PARAMOUNT PICTURES PRESENTS

A ROBERT STIGWOOD/ALLAN CARR PRODUCTION

JOHN TRAVOLTA   OLIVIA NEWTON-JOHN in "GREASE"

and STOCKARD CHANNING as Rizzo with special guest appearances by EVE ARDEN, FRANKIE AVALON

JOAN BLONDELL, EDD BYRNES, SID CAESAR, ALICE GHOSTLEY, DODY GOODMAN, SHA-NA-NA

Screenplay by BRONTE WOODARD   Adaptation by ALLAN CARR   Based on the original musical by JIM JACOBS and WARREN CASEY

Produced on the Broadway Stage by KENNETH WAISSMAN and MAXINE FOX in association with ANTHONY D'AMATO   Choreography — PATRICIA BIRCH

Produced by ROBERT STIGWOOD and ALLAN CARR   Directed by RANDAL KLEISER   DOLBY SYSTEM   PANAVISION   A PARAMOUNT PICTURE

PG PARENTAL GUIDANCE SUGGESTED   Soundtrack Album available on RSO Records & Tapes   Read the paperback from Pocket Books   ©1978 PARAMOUNT PICTURES CORPORATION

SOME MATERIAL MAY NOT BE SUITABLE FOR CHILDREN

780018

279. GREASE, 1978

280. SKATETOWN USA, 1979

281. THE MUPPET MOVIE, 1979

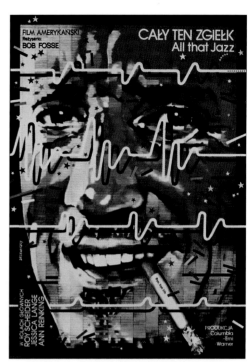

282. ALL THAT JAZZ, 1979, Polish poster

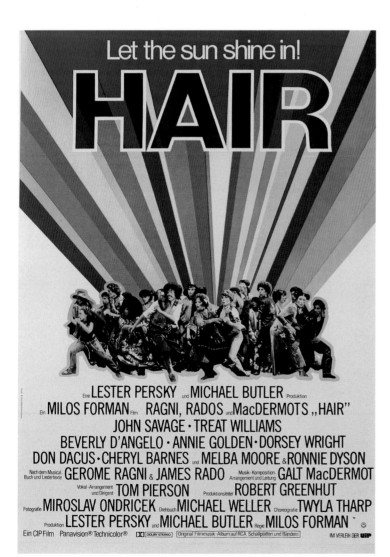

283. HAIR, 1979, German poster

284. THE BLUES BROTHERS, 1980

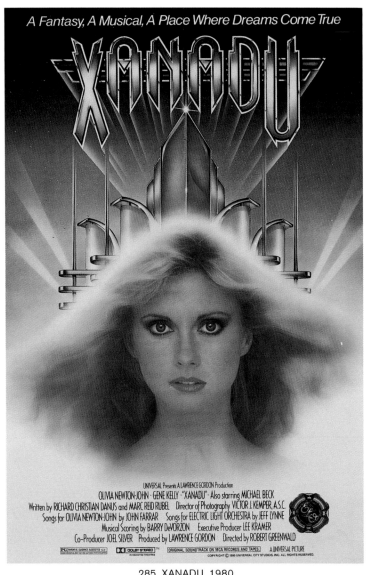

285. XANADU, 1980

286. CAN'T STOP THE MUSIC, 1980

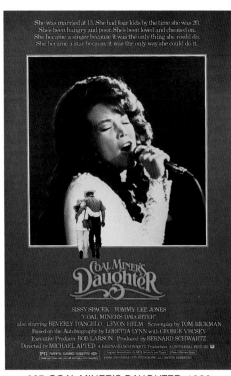

287. COAL MINER'S DAUGHTER, 1980

288. FAME, 1980

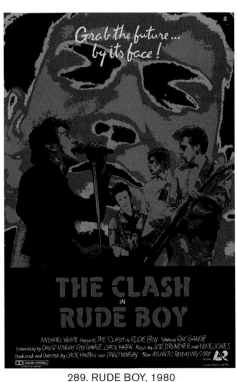

289. RUDE BOY, 1980

290. THE BEST LITTLE WHOREHOUSE IN TEXAS, 1982

291. PENNIES FROM HEAVEN, 1981

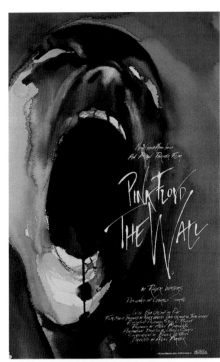

292. THE WALL, 1982

293. STAYING ALIVE, 1983

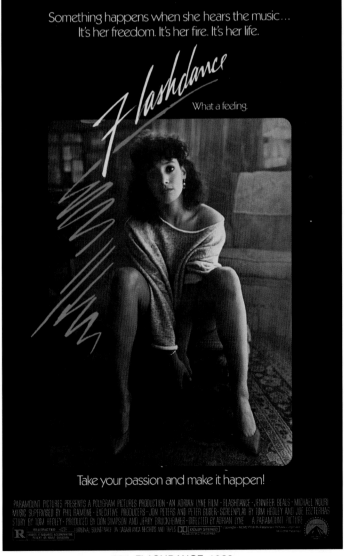

294. FLASHDANCE, 1983

295. HARD TO HOLD, 1984

296. BEAT STREET, 1984

297. BREAKIN', 1984

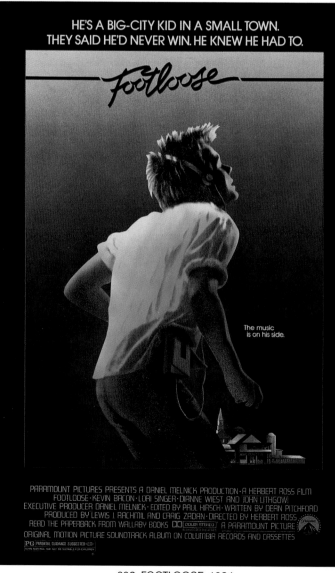

298. FOOTLOOSE, 1984

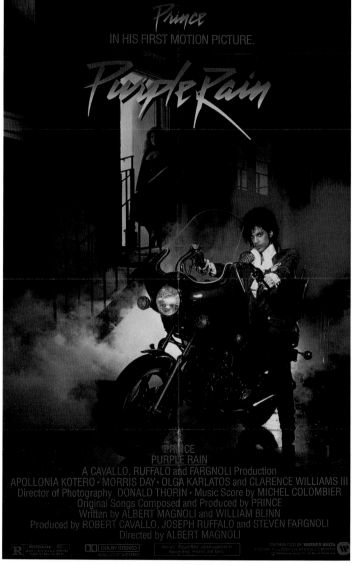

299. PURPLE RAIN, 1984

300. THAT'S DANCING, 1985

301. BRING ON THE NIGHT, 1985

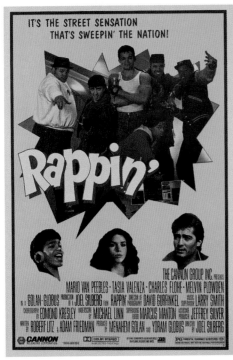

302. RAPPIN', 1985

303. A CHORUS LINE, 1985

304. ABSOLUTE BEGINNERS, 1986

305. ROUND MIDNIGHT, 1986

306. HAIL! HAIL! ROCK 'N' ROLL, 1987

307. LA BAMBA, 1987

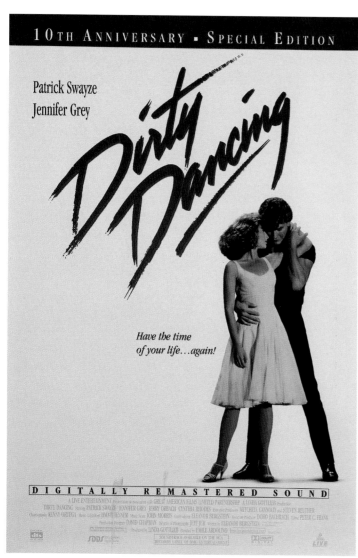

308. DIRTY DANCING, 1987 (1997 reissue)

309. THE MUSIC TEACHER, 1988

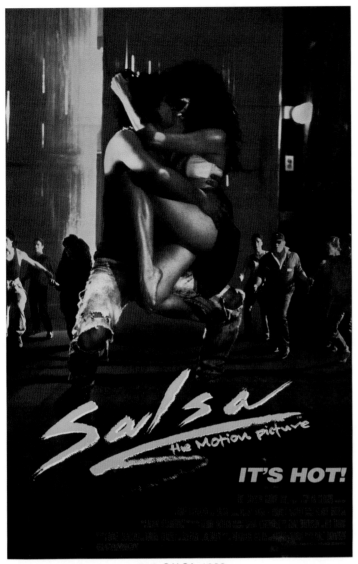

310. SALSA, 1988

311. U2 RATTLE AND HUM, 1988

312. TANGO BAR, 1988

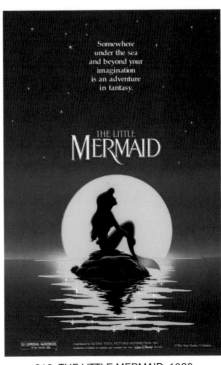

313. THE LITTLE MERMAID, 1989

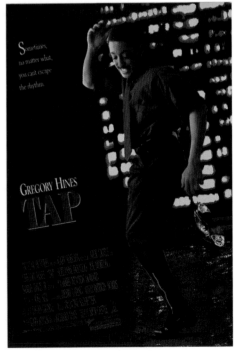

314. TAP, 1989

315. FOR THE BOYS, 1991

316. MO' BETTER BLUES, 1990

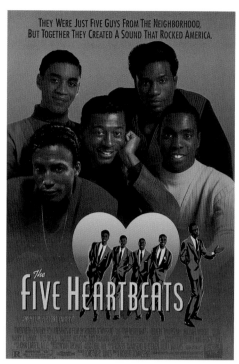

317. THE FIVE HEARTBEATS, 1991

318. THE DOORS, 1991

319. BEAUTY AND THE BEAST, 1991

320. ALADDIN, 1992

321. STRICTLY BALLROOM, 1992

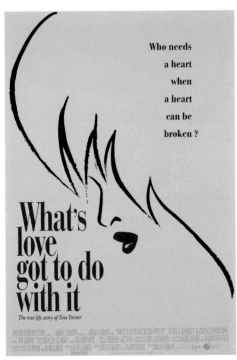

322. WHAT'S LOVE GOT TO DO WITH IT, 1993

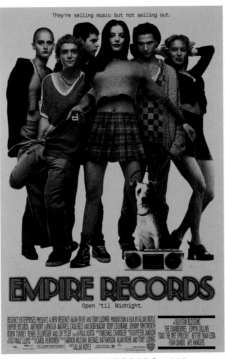

323. EMPIRE RECORDS, 1995

324. EVITA, 1996

325. SHALL WE DANCE, 1997

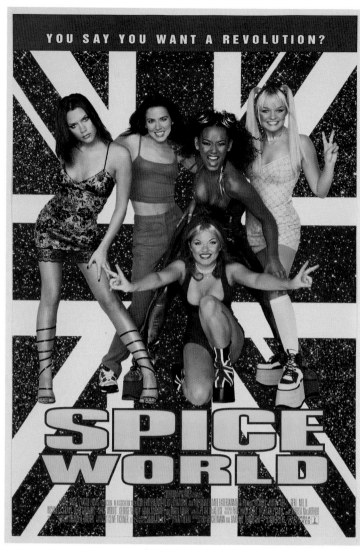

326. SPICE WORLD, 1997

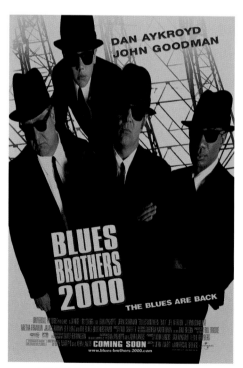

327. BLUES BROTHERS 2000, 1998

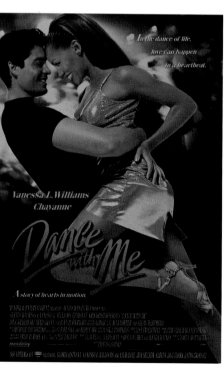

328. DANCE WITH ME, 1998

329. THE KING AND I, 1999

Available August 1999